Trevor Wye

FLUTE CLASS

A GROUP TEACHING BOOK
FOR STUDENTS AND TEACHERS

Piano accompaniments by Robert Scott

The piano part is inserted

Order No: NOV 120738

NOVELLO PUBLISHING LIMITED

PREFACE

This book aims to provide interesting material for those who teach the flute to groups of three or more pupils together.

The sequence of learning new notes follows conventional patterns and the music ventures into no more than two sharps or two flats.

The book contains

- Solos, duets, trios, and quartets, some (marked 'P') with piano accompaniment.
- Four sections on improvisations of varying kinds.
- The scales and arpeggios required for Grades 1, 2, and 3 of the Associated Board of the Royal Schools of Music.
- At the back of the book, fifteen trios and quartets for concert use, some of them incorporating jazz styles and harmonies.
- A separate, and very easy piano part to those pieces marked 'P'.

For additional solo pieces, the 'Very Easy' series of albums with piano accompaniment is recommended (published by Novello). There are two volumes of Baroque music, and one each of Classical, Romantic, and Twentieth-century repertoire.

TREVOR WYE
1992

IMPORTANT!

Each pupil should have his or her own copy of this book so that individual study, practice and rehearsal can continue at home.

Note that, in some parts of the world, different notational terms are used. See page 5 for an American glossary.

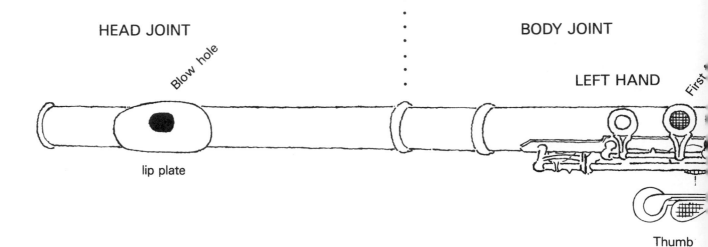

HEAD JOINT

Blow hole

lip plate

BODY JOINT

LEFT HAND

First

Thumb

PREPARATION

Blowing the head joint

Firstly, learn to blow using only the **head joint**.

Place the palm of your right hand across the open end of the tube to make it airtight. Place the **lip plate** against the lower lip so that less than half of the **blow hole** is covered. The head joint is parallel with the lips. Bring your lips together and blow across the hole. Try to keep the tone steady. Start each note with the syllable TWHO.

Once you are successful, assemble the whole flute as in the diagram at the top of the page.

Make sure that the blow hole is in line with the key for the first finger of the left hand. Notice the **foot joint** position.

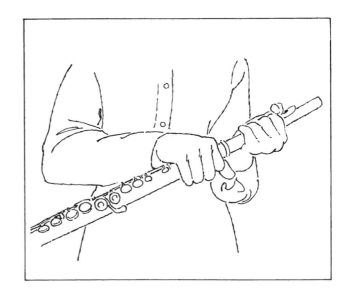

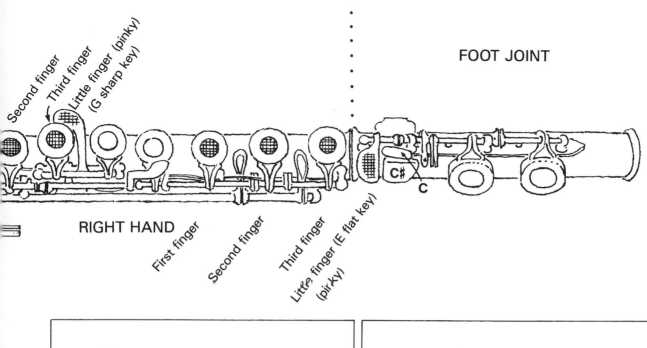

Second finger
Third finger
Little finger (pinky)
(G sharp key)

FOOT JOINT

RIGHT HAND

First finger
Second finger
Third finger
Little finger (E flat key)
(pinky)

C#

C

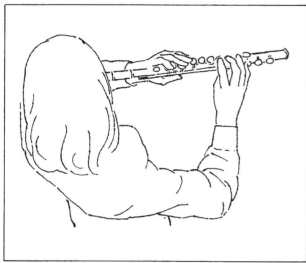

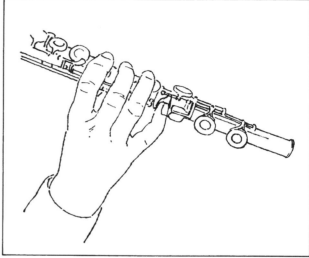

Right hand

Study the pictures above: notice the angle of the flute in relation to the body. Place both hands on the flute as shown in the drawing. Place your right hand fingers as shown and keep the little finger (pinky) curved.

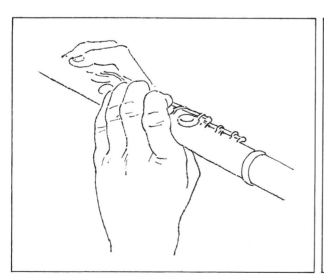

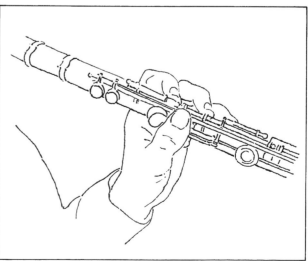

Left hand

The flute is supported at the base of the left hand first finger whilst the fingers curve over the keys. Notice the left hand thumb: keep it on the correct lever.

Blowing the flute

Always stand when playing. Holding the flute in front of you, turn your head about 45 degrees to the left and bring the flute to your head. Avoid bringing your head to the flute. Observe that your head and the flute are facing in a different direction to your shoulders.

This is how the fingering for each note will be shown:

Thumb   Left hand

Little finger   Right hand

●   indicates finger or thumb ON

○   indicates finger or thumb OFF

⌣   put finger on key

Finger the note B: **Left hand first finger and thumb**

Right hand little finger on E flat key

and play your first note:

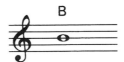

Remember to start each note with your tongue.

Try to relax your arms and shoulders.

► Notation

Musical notes are named after the first seven letters of the alphabet. They are placed on the **stave**:

This sign  is called a **treble clef** and shows that the

instrument playing from the stave is a high or treble instrument, such as the recorder, the violin or the flute.

Music is grouped into **bars** (measures) to show rhythmic stress or accent. The **barline** shows the beginning and end of each bar. The final **double barline** shows the end of a piece of music.

There are several different note lengths in music. Here are some of them:

○ semibreve (whole-note)

♩ minim (half-note)

♩ crotchet (quarter-note)

AMERICAN GLOSSARY

Semibreve	Whole-note	Bar	Measure
Minim	Half-note	Beat	Count
Crotchet	Quarter-note	Little finger	Pinky
Quaver	Eighth-note		
Semiquaver	Sixteenth-note		

STARTING TO PLAY

Take up your flute and play the exercise below counting four crotchet beats (quarter-note counts) in each bar. Play the notes for their full length. You will use only one note: B.

Now play the following piece. It is in the rhythm of *Au Clair de la Lune*, but played only on one note: B.

AU CLAIR DE LA   LU – NE   1 2 3 4
                 1 2 3 4

Now a new note, A, using the rhythm of the tune *Twinkle, Twinkle, Little Star*.

TWIN – KLE TWIN – KLE   LIT – TLE STAR,   HOW I WON–DER

WHAT YOU ARE.

► **Remember to tongue**

Four exercises using the notes B, A, and the new note: G.

6

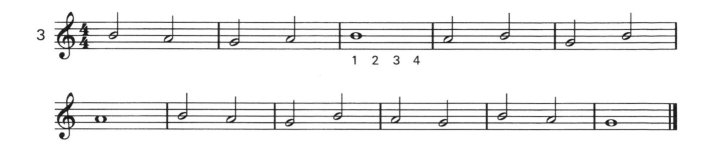

► Rests

There are special signs for silence in music, called **rests**. Here are the rests that correspond to the note lengths you have learned so far:

| semibreve rest | minim rest | crotchet rest |
| (whole-note rest) | (half-note rest) | (quarter-note rest) |

Here is a **duet**:   ► A **duet** is a piece of music in two parts.

Count carefully in this duet:

Au Clair de la Lune as a duet:

MERRILY WE ROLL ALONG

Here is a **trio**, the first of many in this book:

► A **trio** is a piece with three independent parts.

CROSSOVERS

Practise this solo at home. Count carefully.

Bone flute played by North American Indians

INTRODUCING
C

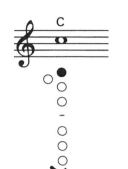

Try not to support the flute with your left thumb when playing C.

► **Slurs**

A **slur** is a curved line placed above or below a group of notes of different pitch.
The notes are played in one breath, tonguing only the first.

AIR DE BUFFONS

16th century

9

► **Time signatures**

A time signature, consisting of two numbers on top of each other, is printed at the beginning of a piece of music to tell you what note values to expect in each bar. So far, you have only played in  time, often called **common**

time and written  instead of (but it means the same).

Here are some new time signatures:

two crotchets in each bar **2/4**

three crotchets in each bar **3/4**

In this next duet, some of the group should click their fingers or clap hands instead of playing. This is indicated by the sign ✳

A tutor who tooted the flute
Tried to tutor two tooters to toot
Said the two to the tutor
Is it easier to toot
Or to tutor two tooters to toot?

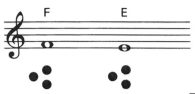
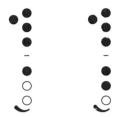

Check your right hand position with the pictures at the front of the book.

► **Repeat signs**

These are **repeat signs**:  When you see them, repeat all the music between the two signs once. If there is only one sign, as in the next piece, repeat from the beginning.

TRIO

PURCELL

► **Dotted notes**

A **dot** after a note lengthens that note by half. So a **dotted minim** (dotted half-note) will be three beats instead of two. This  is the same as

1-2-3 4

TRIO

If there are only two players, play parts I and III.

WALTZ

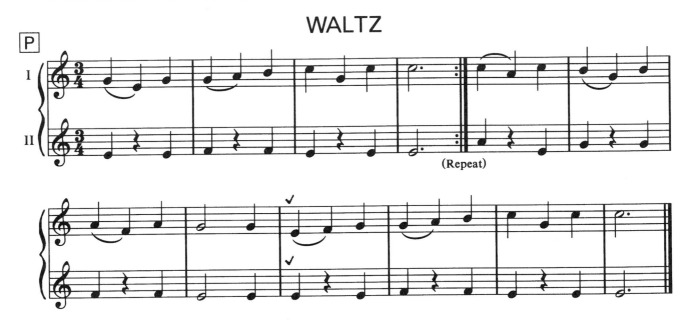

(Repeat)

▶ **Ties**
When two notes of the same pitch are joined together by a curved line, called a **tie**, they are played as one continuous note, or **tied** together.

▶ **Phrasing**
Like speech, music is divided into **phrases**; try to take your breath at places which don't stop the 'flow' of the **phrase**.

In the next piece, there are four phrases.

DUET

The first flutes were made many thousands of years ago out of human bones, the tibia (leg bone) being a favourite. Until fairly recent times, tribes in South America would make flutes out of the bones, and drums out of the skins, of their defeated enemies, upon which to make music both to celebrate their victory and honour their foes.

INTRODUCING
F SHARP

F sharp

The new note is F sharp.

► All notes can be raised, or lowered, by placing a sign in front of them.

The sign for raising a note is called a **sharp**: ♯. Its effect is cancelled by the barline.

1

2

► **Key signatures**

Instead of writing a sharp sign in front of every F in a piece, the sharp is placed at the beginning of each line of music and is called a **key signature**. There are two keys which use the **key signature** of one sharp: G major and E minor.

G major

DANCE

SUSATO

INTRODUCING
QUAVERS
(EIGHTH NOTES)

► There are two **quavers** to every crotchet. Notice the tail: . When two or more **quavers** are grouped together, their tails are joined.

 equals count

1   2 and 3

1 2 & 3 4

DUET

WALTZ

► A piece with no key signature
is either in C major or A minor.

This next piece is in C major.

MUFFINS

The God Pan is playing pan-pipes, another ancient form of the flute. Its invention was thus: Pan fell in love with a beautiful maiden called Syrinx, though she ran away from him and hid in some reeds on a river bank. Pan slashed at the reeds and, not finding her, bound a bunch of canes together to make a flute on which to express his woe. Their love had been uneven, so the length of canes remained uneven: she who was once a beautiful maiden became a musical pipe!

First, play this exercise:

Now repeat it, with the first two notes tied together:

(a)

1 - 2 & 3

► A **dotted crotchet** (dotted quarter-note) is a crotchet plus a quaver. A dot after a note lengthens that note by half its value. A **dotted crotchet** is worth one and a half beats.

(b)

Exercises (a) and (b) should sound exactly the same.

GOD SAVE THE QUEEN (America)

G major

THE MAIDEN

► **First and second time bars**

Sometimes a repeated phrase has a different ending. In this next piece, play the first six bars; then repeat, but the second time through, skip the bar marked 1 and play the second, marked 2, instead.

MELODY

► **Staccato**

A dot placed under or over a note means that it is to be played short, or **staccato**.

BOUNCING

ROAST BEEF

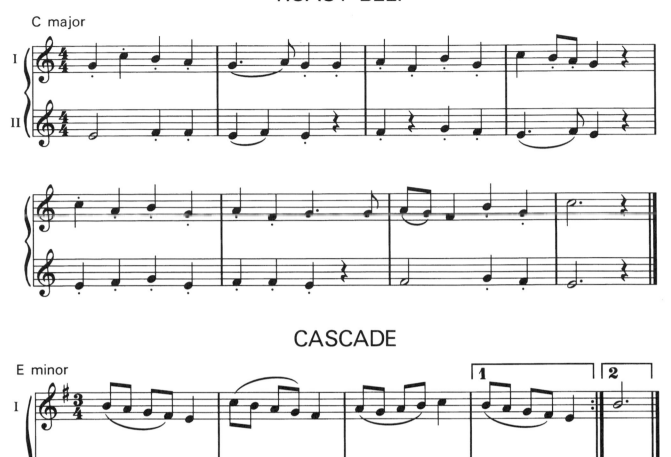

CASCADE

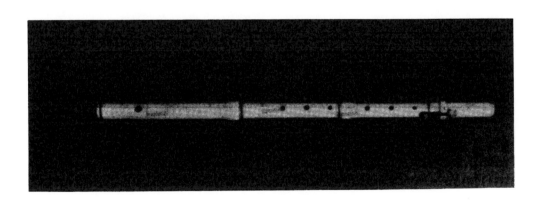

The one-keyed flute. This was the flute used from about 1720. More keys were added between that date and 1830 when Theobald Boehm (see page 80) began his experiments. It has been recently revived, and can be heard at concerts today where it is usually called the Baroque flute, or Flauto Traverso.

INTRODUCING
B FLAT AND D

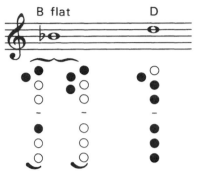

No little finger on key

► The sign for lowering a note is called a **flat**: ♭

The two new notes are B **flat** and D. B **flat** can be played in two ways: the choice of which fingering to use should be made by your teacher.

► A key signature of one **flat** indicates that the piece is either in F major, or D minor.

This next piece is in F major: all B's are played as B flats.

Some interesting sounds can be made without blowing across the flute blow hole:
● Without holding your flute to your mouth, finger G and pat the first finger key of the right hand. It will play a note of about F.

● When you see this sign: pat the key to accompany this trio:

CUCKOO

Tone

The best way to develop a beautiful **tone** is to play long notes by yourself.

● Practise this exercise at home every day.
● Listen to your **tone** when you practise.

► **The pause**

This sign placed over a note indicates that the note is to be held for longer than its value.

TONE EXERCISE

WALTZ

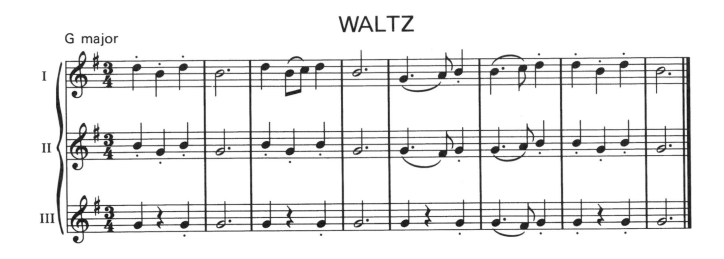

JINGLE BELLS

INTRODUCING
LOW D

Notice that low D is played without *the right hand little finger.*

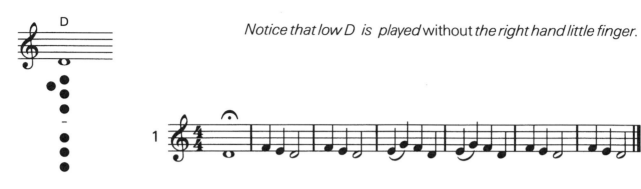

A round

- In the next piece, the first player starts alone;
- when the '2' is reached, the second player starts at the beginning;
- when the first player reaches the '3', the third player starts at the beginning, and so on.

LONDON'S BURNING

TRADITIONAL

The next round can be played by either four or eight players: if four players, follow the figures above the music; if eight players, follow the lower figures.

▶ This piece starts with an incomplete bar. The note before the first barline is called an **upbeat**.

ROUND

► **Musical terms**

The signs and words to show the style, speed, and mood of a piece of music are traditionally written in Italian. From here onwards you will be introduced to the most common words. For reference, there is a list on page 69.

AIR DE BUFFONS

16th century

► A **canon** is a piece in which the second part exactly imitates the first part.

CANON: Noel

Allegro (quickly)

CHEDEVILLE

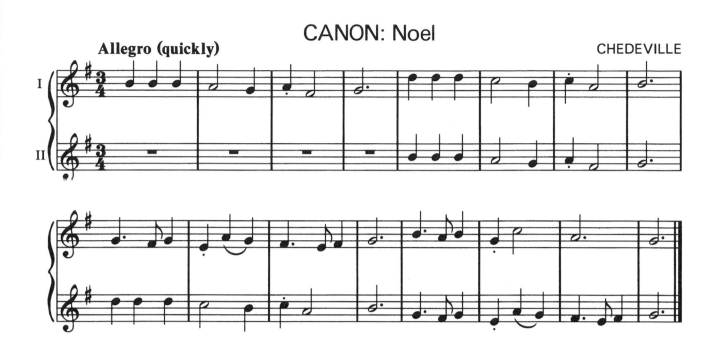

► **The natural sign** ♮

This cancels the effect of a sharp or a flat. A sharp, flat or **natural** occurring within a bar is called an **accidental**; its effect is only temporary and is cancelled by the barline.

GERMAN DANCE

M. FRANCK

INTRODUCING
E, F, AND G

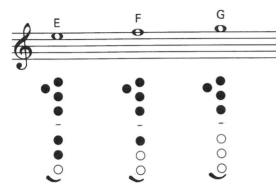

► So far, you have learned some notes between low D and D:  this span of eight notes is called an **octave**. For the new notes E, F, and G in the second octave of the flute, use a faster air speed, or the notes will slip down to the lower octave. Use the same fingering as for the lower octave.

GOOD KING WENCESLAS

IMPROVISATION
1

► Improvisation means making up music as you go along. It is usual in the performance of old music and in jazz.

● One player only should improvise; the rest will provide a **drone**, or accompaniment.

● Divide into an equal number of players to play the drone:

● The 'soloist' should improvise using these notes:

HINTS
● Be clear about the rhythm.
● Remember, you can't play 'wrong' notes when improvising!

The classical Chinese flute, the Tse. Our modern flutes are descended from this simple bamboo flute which has been in use in China for several thousand years.

► **D. C. al Fine**

This is an abbreviation for **Da Capo al Fine** and means go back to the beginning of the piece and play as far as the word 'Fine' or end.

MAYPOLE DANCE

UNTO US A CHILD IS BORN

CAN-CAN

OFFENBACH

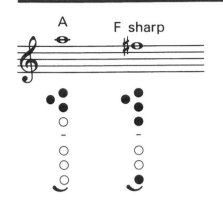

A   F sharp

Both A and F sharp have the same fingering as the same notes in the lower octave.

1

2

DUET

Allegro

I

II

Change parts at the repeat

SAD WALTZ

18th century

P Moderato

I

II

III

1   2

MINUET

J.S. BACH

Allegretto (less quick than allegro)

TWINKLE, TWINKLE

C major

Moderato

INTRODUCING C SHARP

C sharp

When approaching and moving on from C sharp, take care to use your right hand little finger on the key; it helps to keep the correct balance of the flute.

► A key signature of two sharps, F sharp and C sharp, indicates that the piece is in either D major or B minor.

D major

D major

D major

Allegro

► **Scales and arpeggios**
Scales are a series of notes which ascend and descend in ladder-like steps.
Arpeggios are similar but with some of the steps missed out.

Learn to play this **scale** and **arpeggio** from memory.

SCALE OF D MAJOR

ARPEGGIO OF D MAJOR

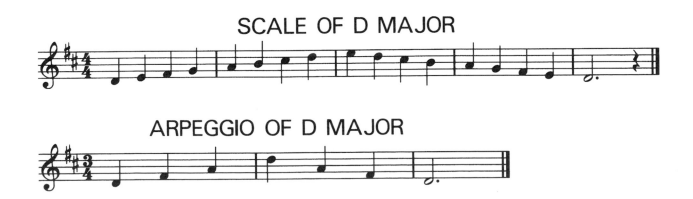

DANCE

D major

HAUPTMANN

Solo means by yourself (an important part).

THE GRENADIER

THE STREETS OF LAREDO

TRADITIONAL

▶ Reminder: Two keys share the key signature of one flat: F major and D minor.

Minor keys have a different musical flavour to major keys. This piece is in D minor.

DANISH FOLK SONG

ROUND: Come follow me

J. HILTON

F major
Andante

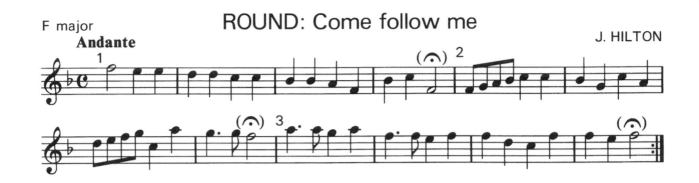

A TRICKY DUET

Andantino

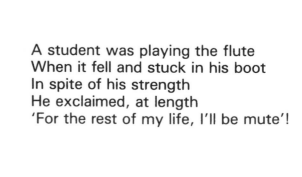

A student was playing the flute
When it fell and stuck in his boot
In spite of his strength
He exclaimed, at length
'For the rest of my life, I'll be mute'!

INTRODUCING
G SHARP

The left hand little finger is used for the first time.

► Reminder: A key signature of no sharps or flats indicates that the piece is either in C major, or A minor. This next piece is in A minor.

OLD FRENCH CAROL

The scale and arpeggio of A minor:

A minor

► Trills

A **trill** is a decoration and its sign is shown as  Bounce

your finger on the F sharp key two or three times so as to alternate between
F sharp and G for the duration of the note.

A solo with piano accompaniment:

WALTZ

SCHUBERT

GAVOTTE

LOEILLET
(pronounced LE(R)-EE-AY)

► Accent

The sign for an **accent** is this symbol ➤ placed above or below a note.
It means that the note is given emphasis, or an **accent**.

These two notes are fingered the same as B and C in the lower octave.

1

2

► **Triplets**

A **triplet** is a group of three notes played in the time of two notes of the same value. For instance, a **triplet** of three quavers would be played in the time of two quavers. **Triplets** are shown by the figure 3 placed above or below them.

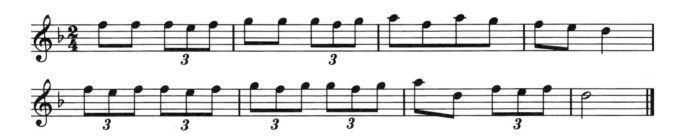

► **Tenuto**

The sign for a **tenuto** accent is a short line placed above or below a note. The word **tenuto** means 'held' so that the note must be played for its full value and not shortened. It must also be played with a gentle accent.

► **Expression in music**

Italian words are used to indicate how a piece is to be played. Here are the words and the abbreviations you will find in your music:

p	or	*piano*	soft
f	or	*forte*	loud
mp	or	*mezzo piano*	half or moderately soft
mf	or	*mezzo forte*	half or moderately loud
>	or	*diminuendo*	becoming softer
<	or	*crescendo*	becoming louder

CUCKOOS

INTRODUCING QUAVER RESTS
(EIGHTH-NOTE RESTS)

► Quavers have their own signs for rests:

The rest lasts for half a crotchet beat.

ROUND: Fay, may prithee John

ANONYMOUS

INTRODUCING
LOUD AND SOFT PLAYING

The signs for loud and soft playing, *forte* and *piano*, are important for creating expression in music — but you may have noticed that, when playing loudly, the note goes sharp; when playing softly, it goes flat. To counteract this tuning problem, in *piano* or soft playing raise the air stream by bringing your jaw forward; in *forte* or loud playing bring your jaw back.

The jaw moves gradually and smoothly back in *crescendo*, and forward in *diminuendo*.

TAMBOURIN

RAMEAU

D.C. al Fine

► **Scales and arpeggios**

There are two forms of minor scale: **harmonic** and **melodic**. For examination purposes, you will need to know both forms which are printed here.

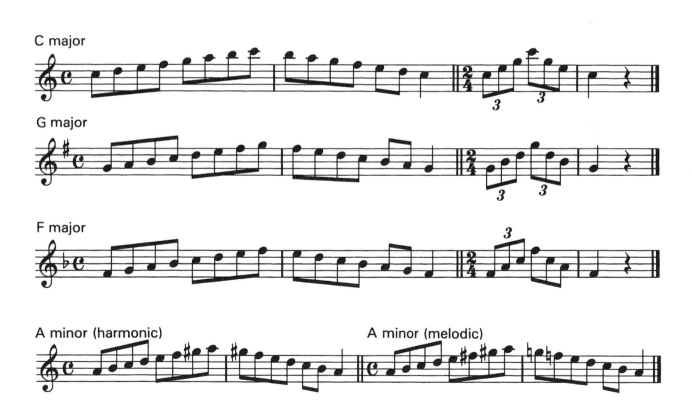

C major

G major

F major

A minor (harmonic)   A minor (melodic)

The arpeggio for both forms of minor scale stays the same:

A minor

RUSSIAN SONG

THE ASH GROVE

44

INTRODUCING
B FLAT

B flat has the same fingering as the B flat in the lower octave.

1

INTRODUCING
COMPOUND TIME

▶ When the pulse or beat of a piece can be divided into three, the music is said to be in **compound time**. $\frac{6}{8}$ is one example: it has two dotted crotchet beats in each bar. There are three quavers in each dotted crotchet.

In exercise 2, count two beats in each bar: in bar 3 think of the word CO-VEN-TRY to help you play the correct rhythm.

In exercise 3, the second and third bars should sound exactly the same as each other.

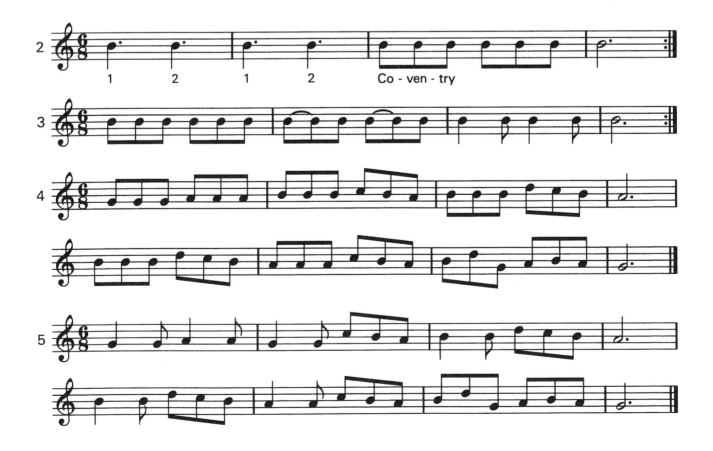

DUET: I saw three ships

PLAISIR D'AMOUR

MARTINI

INTRODUCING
E FLAT

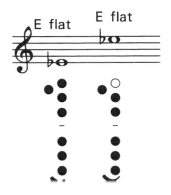

E flat   E flat

▶ These next pieces also introduce a new key signature of two flats which can be either B flat major or G minor.

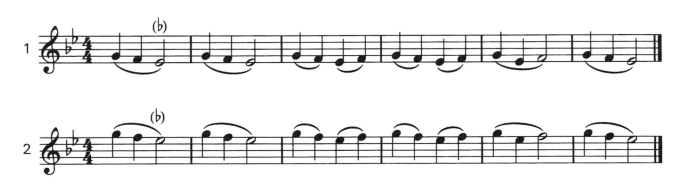

1

2

FAREWELL

B flat major

Mesto (sadly)

I

II

III

DUET

FIRST PART

SECOND PART

DUET

The players of the second part will turn their book upside down!

Scales and arpeggios

B flat major

G minor (harmonic)

G minor (melodic)

► **Bars' rests**

Sometimes, a piece of music contains several bars' rests in a row, shown by ├───────┤ with the appropriate figure above it:

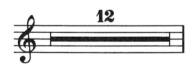

48

In this trio, the rests are written out in full.

SOUVENIR DE GAND

B flat major

SEGHERS

► Music is a language in which phrases have endings called **cadences**. A **cadence** is the last two chords in a phrase.

- Two players should play parts 1 and 2, and keep repeating the two bars without stopping.
- The remainder of the group can, in turn, improvise or invent endings to fit the harmony.
- The two repeating parts can be played on a piano or synthesizer if available.

EXAMPLES:

TONE EXERCISE

Practise this tone exercise for a few minutes each day. Use your lip muscles to focus the tone and make it clear and bright.

FINGER TWISTER

INTRODUCING
NEW NAMES FOR OLD NOTES

► You have just learned E flat, which is an E *lowered* by a **semitone**. Another name for E flat is D sharp, that is, D *raised* by a semitone. All the notes learned so far have double names:

F sharp is the same as G flat

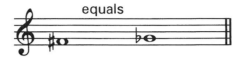

C sharp is the same as D flat

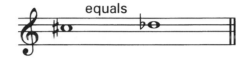

G sharp is the same as **A** flat

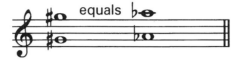

B flat is the same as A sharp

Exercise:

Exercise 2 is a **chromatic** scale.

► The word '**chromatic**' means *all* colours, or notes.

51

D major

DUET

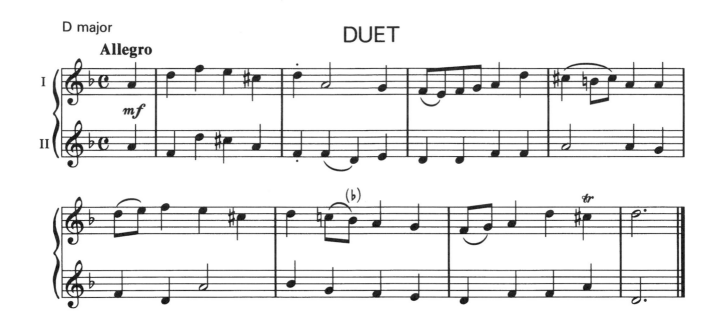

THE AQUARIUM

E minor

SAINT-SAËNS

INTRODUCING
UPPER C SHARP AND D

WALTZ

D major

SCHUBERT

Con moto (with motion)

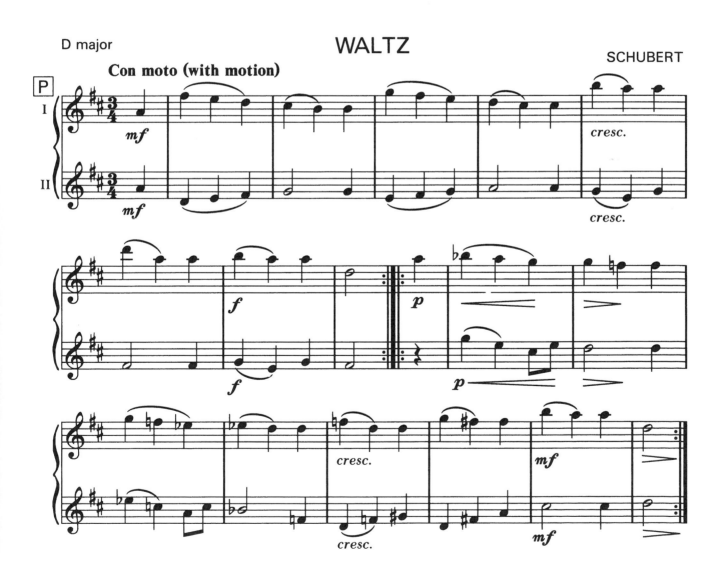

Scales and arpeggios

Here are the scale and arpeggio requirements for the Associated Board Grade 2 examination:

D minor melodic

OR

The arpeggio for both the harmonic and the melodic version of a minor scale is the same.

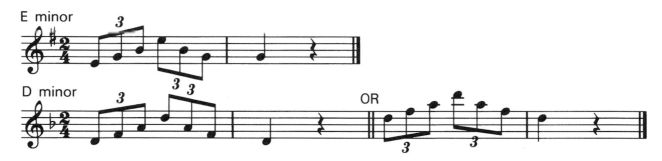

E minor

D minor

OR

► Acciaccaturas

Music is sometimes decorated by small notes and other signs often called grace notes or ornaments. One of these grace notes, the **acciaccatura**, has a long name for a note to be played as quickly as possible, squeezed in before the note which follows.

JOHN PEEL

Presto (very quickly)

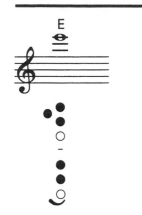

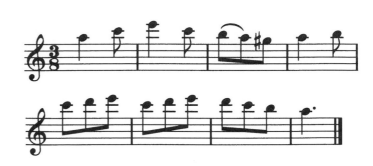

► Here is a new time signature $\frac{3}{8}$ which has three quaver beats in each bar.

COVENTRY CAROL

A minor

Allegretto semplice (simply)

INTRODUCING
SEMIQUAVERS
(SIXTEENTH-NOTES)

► A quaver may be divided into two **semiquavers** ♪♪ or ♫ The tails of each of two or more semiquavers are joined together to make reading easier. A crotchet can be made up of

Allegro in unison (all together)

A REEL

THE DRUNKEN SAILOR

TRADITIONAL

INTRODUCING
TOP E FLAT AND F

O LITTLE ONE SWEET

17th century

INTRODUCING SYNCOPATION

► When the beat falls in the middle of a note, it is said to be **syncopated**. **Syncopation** adds a bouncy and sometimes 'jazzy' quality to the music.

Play the first exercise quickly; then follow it with the second which has two beats in a bar. The two performances should sound the same.

IMPROVISATION
3

Here is another chord sequence to improvise upon, with some examples:*

EXAMPLES:

*For further examples and hints on how to improvise see *A Trevor Wye Practice Book for the Flute*, Volume 5 (Novello).

SCOTCH DANCE

BEETHOVEN

I SAW THREE SHIPS

UNISON (all together)

INTRODUCING
TOP F SHARP AND G

F sharp   G

▶ The air speed will need to be increased for these upper notes. They become easier with practice.

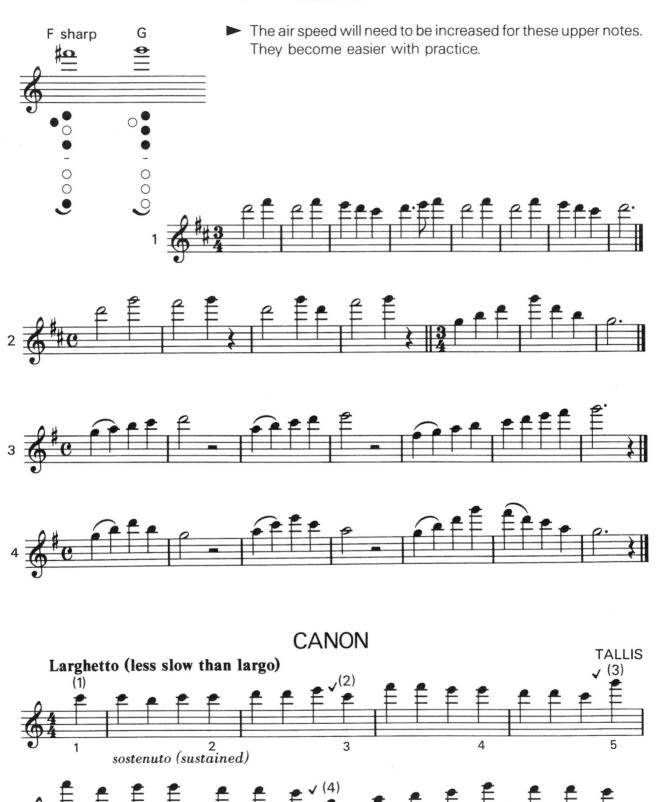

CANON

TALLIS

Larghetto (less slow than largo)

sostenuto (sustained)

RIGADOON

PURCELL

You have played this melody before an octave lower.

MINUET

BACH

INTRODUCING
DOTTED QUAVERS
(DOTTED EIGHTH-NOTES)

► A **dotted quaver** lasts half as long again as a quaver. It normally has a semiquaver attached to it to complete the beat.

First, play *Dot's Tune* quickly, two minim beats in each bar:

DOT'S TUNE

Now play it again in $\frac{2}{4}$ time. The two performances should sound the same. To help with the rhythm, think of the words ONCE A-GAIN.

once a-gain

GREENSLEEVES

ANON

INTRODUCING MULTIPHONICS

► In modern music, flute players are often asked to play more than one note at a time. These **multiphonics** are quite easy. Here are two for you to try: *

This is fingered like top D, but blow more loosely to get the double note.

Finger F and, at the same time, put down both trill keys, blow gently and with relaxed lips. When you can do it, try this waltz accompaniment:

Waltz time

*Both these multiphonics are used in *A Very Easy Twentieth-Century Album* (Novello).

INTRODUCING THE REMAINING NOTES

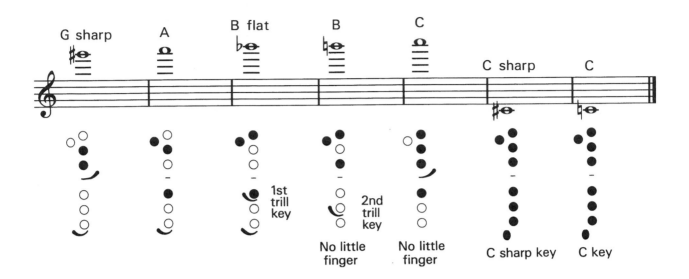

IMPROVISATION
4

Instead of having a chord on which to play an improvisation, it can be done freely, using an idea, or a subject.

- Try improvising just using one of the subjects below; then try improvising on your own subject.

A storm   Ducks   A haunted house   Boiled eggs   Anger   The Queen   Itchy feet
School dinners   Cycling   A traffic jam   Rain   A disco   Roses   Flying   A flat tyre

- Or you could play a 'portrait' of one member of your group.

You don't necessarily need to 'blow' the flute when improvising: some interesting sounds to help you create your picture can be made by
- patting the keys;
- breathing gently down the flute, with your mouth completely covering the blow hole;
- using only the headjoint (try pushing your finger in and out of the end while blowing).

Or write out a piece of your own composition, 8 bars long, that you would play at a concert.

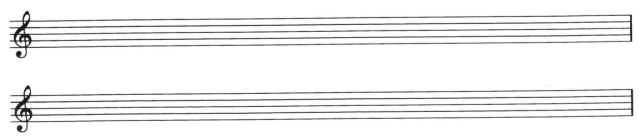

Remember the key signature and time signature!

SCALES AND ARPEGGIOS

Here are the scale and arpeggio requirements for the Associated Board Grade 3 examination. They are all to be played both tongued and *legato*.

E minor

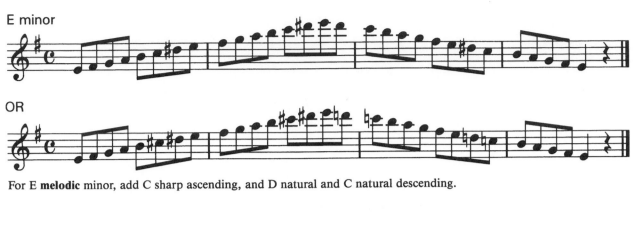

OR

For E **melodic** minor, add C sharp ascending, and D natural and C natural descending.

B minor

D minor

G minor

G chromatic

A LIST OF ITALIAN WORDS
AND THEIR MEANINGS

Al Fine	to the finish, or the end of a piece, after D. C.
Allegretto	less quickly than *Allegro*
Allegro	quickly
Andante	easy-going (at a moderate walking pace)
Andantino	less slow than *Andante* (some composers use it to mean less **fast** than *Andante*; use your own judgement)
Animato	animated
A tempo	in time (after slowing down)
Cantabile	In a singing style
Con	with
Con moto	with motion
Con spirito	with spirit
Crescendo (cresc.)	gradually getting louder
D.C. (da capo)	go back to the beginning
Diminuendo (dim.)	gradually getting softer
Dolce	sweetly
Fine	the finish, or end
Forte (f)	loudly
Grazioso	gracefully
Larghetto	less slowly than *Largo*
Largo	slowly and broadly
Leggiero	lightly
Legato	smoothly
Maestoso	majestically
Mesto	sadly
Mezzo forte (mf)	half or moderately loud
Mezzo piano (mp)	half or moderately soft
Moderato	at a moderate speed
Piano	softly
Rallentando (rall.)	gradually getting slower
Ritenuto (rit.)	slower
Simile	continue in the same way
Sonore	with a full rich tone
Sostenuto	sustained
Tempo	time
Tempo di minuetto	in the time of a minuet
Tempo di valse	in waltz time
Vivace	lively
Vivo	very quickly and lively

CANON: Ding Dong Bell

ANONYMOUS

► Grace Notes. Sometimes a note can have two or more attached to it. They are to be played quickly.

THE HARVESTERS

COUPERIN

SISTER MONICA

COUPERIN

CANON: In drinking

J. CLARKE

RONDO

SUSATO

DING DONG! MERRILY ON HIGH

16th century

ESTILO

G minor

LATIN AMERICAN FOLK SONG

MANGO WALK

TRADITIONAL

ALLEMANDE

Allegretto pomposo (pompously)

GERVAISE

76

GOD REST YE MERRY, GENTLEMEN

WELCH RICHARD

TRADITIONAL

RAGGY FLUTES

SMOOTH FLUTES

WYE

BRANLE

GERVAISE

Allegretto giocoso (with humour)

RONDO

SUSATO

DANCE

Giocoso

PRAETORIUS

TREVOR WYE

VIDEO

PLAY THE FLUTE
A beginner's guide

TUTORS

A BEGINNER'S BOOK FOR THE FLUTE
Part 1
Part 2
Piano Accompaniment

PRACTICE BOOKS FOR THE FLUTE
VOLUME 1 Tone
VOLUME 2 Technique
VOLUME 3 Articulation
VOLUME 4 Intonation and Vibrato
VOLUME 5 Breathing and Scales
VOLUME 6 Advanced Practice

A PICCOLO PRACTICE BOOK

PROPER FLUTE PLAYING

SOLO FLUTE

MUSIC FOR SOLO FLUTE

ARRANGEMENTS FOR FLUTE & PIANO

A COUPERIN ALBUM
AN ELGAR FLUTE ALBUM
A FAURE FLUTE ALBUM
A RAMEAU ALBUM
A SATIE FLUTE ALBUM
A SCHUMANN FLUTE ALBUM
A VIVALDI ALBUM

A FIRST LATIN-AMERICAN FLUTE ALBUM
A SECOND LATIN-AMERICAN FLUTE ALBUM

MOZART FLUTE CONCERTO IN G K.313
MOZART FLUTE CONCERTO IN D K.314 AND ANDANTE IN C K.315

SCHUBERT THEME AND VARIATIONS D 935 No. 3

FLUTE ENSEMBLE

THREE BRILLIANT SHOWPIECES

MUSIC FOR FLUTE

TUTORS

WYE, Trevor
A BEGINNER'S BOOK FOR THE FLUTE
A PRACTICE BOOK FOR THE FLUTE:
VOLUME 1 Tone (Cassette also available)
VOLUME 2 Technique
VOLUME 3 Articulation
VOLUME 4 Intonation and vibrato
VOLUME 5 Breathing and scales
VOLUME 6 Advanced Practice
PROPER FLUTE PLAYING

SOLO

ALBUM
ed Trevor Wye
MUSIC FOR SOLO FLUTE
This attractive collection draws together under
one cover 11 major works representing the
fundamental solo flute repertoire, edited in a
clear and practical form.

trans Gordon Saunders
EIGHT TRADITIONAL JAPANESE PIECES
Gordon Saunders has selected and transcribed
these pieces for tenor recorder solo or flute from
the traditional folk music of Japan.

FLUTE AND PIANO

ALBUMS
arr Barrie Carson Turner
CHRISTMAS FUN BOOK
CLASSICAL POPS FUN BOOK
ITALIAN OPERA FUN BOOK
MOZART FUN BOOK
POP CANTATA FUN BOOK
POPULAR CLASSICS FUN BOOK
RAGTIME FUN BOOK
TV THEME FUN BOOK

arr Trevor Wye
A VERY EASY BAROQUE ALBUM, Vols. 1 & 2
A VERY EASY CLASSICAL ALBUM
A VERY EASY ROMANTIC ALBUM
A VERY EASY 20TH CENTURY ALBUM
A FIRST LATIN-AMERICAN FLUTE ALBUM
A SECOND LATIN-AMERICAN FLUTE ALBUM

BENNETT, Richard Rodney
SUMMER MUSIC

COUPERIN, François
arr Trevor Wye
A COUPERIN ALBUM

ELGAR, Edward
arr Trevor Wye
AN ELGAR FLUTE ALBUM

FRASER, Shena
SONATINA

GALWAY, James
THE MAGIC FLUTE OF JAMES GALWAY
SHOWPIECES

HARRIS, Paul
CLOWNS

HURD, Michael
SONATINA

McCABE, John
PORTRAITS

RAMEAU, Jean Philippe
arr Trevor Wye
A RAMEAU ALBUM

REEMAN, John
SIX FOR ONE

SATIE, Erik
arr Trevor Wye
A SATIE FLUTE ALBUM

SCHUBERT, Franz
arr Trevor Wye
THEME AND VARIATIONS D.935 No.3

SCHURMANN, Gerard
SONATINA

VIVALDI, Antonio
arr Trevor Wye
A VIVALDI ALBUM